Par and Yardage

Hole	Par	Yardage	Hole	Par	Yardage
1	4	402	10	4	466
2	3	235	11	4	415
3	4	455	12	3	187
4	4	434	13	4	461
5	4	407	14	4	439
6	4	475	15	5	583
7	3	174	16	4	441
8	4	362	17	4	480
9	5	607	18	3	190
	35	3,551		35	3,662
				70	7,213

97th
U.S. Open
Congressional
Country Club

Writer
Robert Sommers

Photographers
Michael Cohen
Fred Vuich

Editor
Bev Norwood

ISBN 1-878843-19-2

Statistics produced by Unisys Corporation

Published by International Merchandising Corporation,
One Erieview Plaza, Cleveland, Ohio 44114

Designed and produced by Davis Design

Printed in the United States of America

**97th
U.S. Open**

Official Annual Presented by

ROLEX

It was certainly appropriate that our national championship of golf return to an established venue in the nation's capital after an absence of more than three decades, and the June week at Congressional Country Club this year upheld that decision of the United States Golf Association. Congressional provided the usual nail-biting finish and validated the status of Ernie Els as a top-echelon player on the world scene.

Any success Els achieves does not surprise me. I like to think that I "discovered" Ernie for American golf when I played with him for two rounds in the 1992 PGA Championship and immediately invited him to play the following March in my Bay Hill Invitational on the PGA Tour. He had all the marks then, at age 22, of a coming star, and he has proved to be just that during the intervening years.

At Congressional, Els stood up to the challenges of Tom Lehman, the reigning British Open champion, and, with Tiger Woods, the top Americans in the World Ranking; Colin Montgomerie, clearly Europe's No. 1 player at the present time, and Jeff Maggert, one of the more talented men on the PGA Tour, to win his second U.S. Open title.

I hope that you will enjoy this chronicle of the 1997 U.S. Open, a gift to the game by the fine people at Rolex Watch USA. At the direction of Rolex, the proceeds realized from the sale of this book will go to the USGA Members Program for the benefit of junior golf.

Arnold Palmer

From its headwaters in the Allegheny Mountains, the Potomac River flows nearly 300 miles past a chain of historic sites before it empties into the Chesapeake Bay, draining and forming boundaries of portions of Maryland, Virginia and West Virginia. It is a historic river. It breaks through the Blue Ridge Mountains near Harpers Ferry, West Virginia, where in 1859 the abolitionist John Brown seized an Army arsenal in one of the acts leading up to the Civil War; sweeps past Washington D.C., separating the capital from its Virginia suburbs; past Mount Vernon, George Washington's home, then runs another 115 miles before emptying into the bay.

The Civil War can never be forgotten along this river. The Potomac separated the Confederacy from the Union, and now, directly facing one another across its banks, sit memorials to two principal figures of that war. The Lincoln Memorial, on the Washington side, looks across Memorial Bridge toward the broad lawns of Arlington National Cemetery and the Lee-Custis Mansion, the home of Robert E. Lee, on the Virginia side.

No more than 12 or 15 miles upstream, Congressional Country Club occupies high ground above the river's Maryland shore. Although hardly as historic as other river sites, in its own way Congressional has seen conflicts at least as spirited although far less deadly than the Civil War.

An alternate, Steve Hart of Jupiter, Florida, had the honor as first off the tee in the 97th U.S. Open.

The 1997 United States Open was the sixth national golf championship decided on its grounds. Thirty-three years earlier, in what ranks among the club's, and indeed the Open's, most memorable and melodramatic moments, Ken Venturi, only a breath or two from exhaustion, walked ever so slowly toward the final green, holed a nice putt to save his par, and etched his name into the roll of Open champions.

Congressional was just 40 years old then, playing what in effect was its third course. Founded in the early 1920s, the club had been conceived for grand purposes. Joseph H. Himes, a congressman who served as the club's first president, anticipated informal meetings in its Governors' Room among high-ranking government officials who, he expected, would "become acquainted, exchange views, perhaps work out plans for the adjustment and settlement of national and world problems."

Considering the early membership, Himes' vision seemed eminently possible. The rolls would have caused a modern club developer to choke. From politics came Calvin Coolidge, the sitting President; Warren Harding, his predecessor; Herbert Hoover, his successor, and William Howard Taft, the first President known to play golf, who served from 1909 until 1913.

From commerce came John D. Rockefeller Sr. and Jr., John G. Pew, Harry Sinclair, Harvey Firestone, T.A. Mellon, William Randolph Hearst, Alfred, Irenee, Lamont and Pierre duPont, Gustave Pabst, William G. Carnegie, Eugene G. Grace, Walter Chrysler and Vincent Astor.

Just to break the monotony, from the theater came Charlie Chaplin and Ernestine Schumann-Heink, the Prague-born contralto perhaps best known for an endless series of farewell tours. So far as anyone knows, Madame Schumann-Heink never once lifted a golf club in anger.

To accommodate a membership of such grandeur, the founders authorized a clubhouse of commanding presence, a white stucco structure with a red tiled roof perched on the highest hill of the property. It has outdoor and indoor swimming pools, grill rooms, banquet rooms, apartments, bedrooms, and at one time a system of secret passages behind walls of its upper floors that led from bedrooms to conference rooms. It must have been unsettling to be seated in serious debate as a wall parted and Mr. Hoover stepped through the woodwork.

Obviously some of the scenes Himes pictured actually came true, because Congressional did indeed attract titans of government, both elected and appointed. A few weeks before the 1964 Open, a USGA official was allowed to peek through a door of a private dining room as the nine justices of the United States Supreme Court lunched together.

Its wealthy and influential membership notwithstanding, Congressional went through some hard times during the Depression years of the 1930s. Remote from downtown Washington, about 15 miles from the Capitol and reachable only by narrow roads, the membership dwindled steadily. The club was probably saved by the Second World War. When the Office of Strategic Services, the parent of the Central Intelligence Agency, needed secluded grounds to train men for clandestine operations, it rented Congressional's undeveloped grounds for $4,000 a month.

Preparing for actions behind enemy lines, hundreds of agents trained in parachute jumping, espionage and sabotage. Frenchmen, Norwegians, Italians, Greeks and Slavs primed themselves to return home and lead resistance groups. Americans practiced parachuting into China and Europe.

At 607 yards, Congressional's ninth hole was one of the longest in U.S. Open history.

The pond protecting the front of the 18th green provided a scenic view.

Not all of them survived the rigorous, real-life exercises. Machine guns shooting live bullets set up on the ground between the current 14th green and 15th tee killed two trainees. Learning to crawl under the line of fire, one man leaped away from a snake directly into a burst of bullets.

The rent money dried up with the end of the war, but the economy boomed, new roads brought the club closer to the city, and Congressional became solvent once more.

As it is with any club, the centerpiece was the golf course. Laid out first by Devereaux Emmett, one of the period's more prominent golf course architects, it opened in 1924. Six years later Donald Ross worked some revisions, mainly in bunkering.

The original course was pleasant enough but hardly up to U.S. Open standards. Gay Brewer won the 1949 Junior Amateur over the original by beating Mason Rudolph in the final, but sensing it had become obsolete, the membership brought in Robert Trent Jones to build a third nine in time for the 1959 Women's Amateur. Barbara McIntire beat Joanne Goodwin in the final.

Jones returned later to rebuild the first nine of the original in time for the 1964 Open. It seemed to play well then, but many of Jones' greens sat well above the drive zones, a circumstance that became a problem for P.J. Boatwright, the USGA's man who in later years set up Open courses and influenced where the championship would be played. After playing the course during the 1980s in response to a request to consider Congressional for a future Open, Boatwright turned it down, because, he said, Congressional had too many blind shots; landing areas couldn't be seen from the tees of too many holes, and many green surfaces couldn't be seen from the drive zones.

Determined to correct the problems, Congressional then brought in Rees Jones, Trent's youngest son, to work the same wonders he had performed at The Country Club for the 1988 Open and at Hazeltine for the 1991 championship. The club expected only minor adjustments, but Jones agreed with Boatwright about the blind holes and instead proposed what amounted to rebuilding the course completely. The club agreed.

Rees kept the old routing, but by moving massive volumes of earth he lowered some fairways and greens and raised oth-

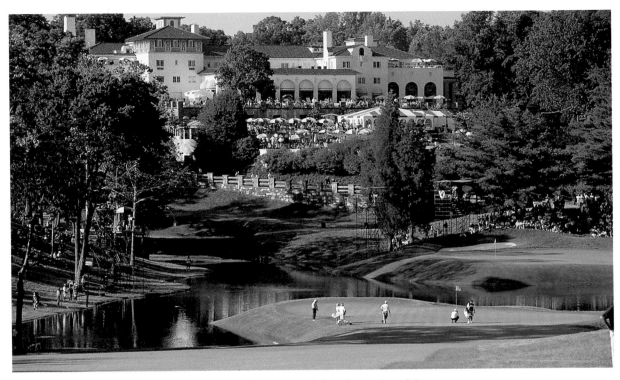

The 17th and 18th holes would be focal points of the championship.

ers, rebuilt every green, and re-bunkered both fairways and greens. When he finished, every landing zone could be seen from every tee, and every green could be seen from the landing zone. The second green was lowered substantially, the fourth fairway elevated to eliminate a blind drive, the sixth green raised, the seventh tee raised and the green lowered, the 12th tee raised eight feet and the green lowered, and he created new tees for the 18th, the Open's first par-three finishing hole since 1909 at the Englewood, New Jersey, Golf Club.

Measuring 190 yards, the home hole called for only a medium iron, but with its green projecting into a broad pond, the new tees brought the tee shots, all carry across the pond, in on a slight angle, creating a narrow target. Jones lowered this green as well and shaved the grass along its side so that anything that missed would probably tumble into the water.

Responding to the tremendous distances the modern golfer of championship quality hits the ball, Jones added new tees that lengthened Congressional to a forbidding 7,213 yards, the longest Open course ever and probably the longest any of the four principal tournaments have been played over.

Nothing unusual in that, though; his father, Trent, had stretched Congressional to 7,053 yards, longest ever in 1964, and the following year lengthened Bellerive Country Club to 7,191 yards.

At first glance Congressional's configuration appeared daunting. Five of its 12 par-four holes measured more than 450 yards, the 17th stretched 480 yards and the sixth 475, and its two par-fives measured 607 and 583 yards. Along with the sixth, the 10th normally played slightly longer for members as a par-five.

Nor were the par-threes pushovers. The second measured 235 yards.

As Rees Jones rebuilt it, Congressional became a first-class test of golf for players of Open caliber. It was severe in the extreme, with narrow fairways, punishing rough and slick greens, but every problem lay open to the players; it was up to them to play it as best they could.

An extraordinary incident took place at Congressional Country Club on June 10, two days before the U.S. Open Championship began. Tiger Woods sat for a mass press interview.

Nothing unusual in that; ever since Woods joined the professional tour he's done the same thing before every tournament he played. Nevertheless, this conference was exceptional for a number of reasons:

• The size of the audience. The press interview area held 280 seats; every one was taken and many other reporters, columnists, and radio and television commentators stood behind the chairs and along the sides of the room. An estimated 350 people attended.

Woods had all the right answers.

• Thirty-three television cameras recorded the moment.

• The interview lasted 45 minutes, from 1 p.m. until 1:45 p.m., about as long as the winner is normally kept.

• The CNN-SI and Golf Channel television networks carried every minute.

• Because press headquarters, set up in Congressional's expansive indoor tennis courts, was so far from the clubhouse, players were driven to the building and back again. As Woods left his interview, seven other television cameras and a number of still photographers shot him climbing into the car.

• Earlier in the day Steve Jones, the

A huge media contingent was on hand for Tiger Woods on Tuesday afternoon.

defending champion, appeared for an interview. Forty reporters sat in the audience.

• An hour or so after Woods left, Justin Leonard came to the press facility. Leonard had just won the tournament at Avenel, just down River Road from Congressional. Seven people waited for him, a turnout so low USGA staffers scurried through the working press area urging writers into the interview room to avoid embarrassing Leonard.

Otherwise:

• Woods came to the interview after playing a practice round. As he stepped onto the first tee, his fans had encircled the hole, and stood seven and eight deep in places outside the gallery ropes.

• Colin Montgomerie led the first round with 65, five under a really difficult par. Woods shot 72. That evening, in the lobby of the hotel that housed most of the press, a group of reporters spoke not of Montgomerie's marvelous round but of Woods' refusal of another mass interview. In the dining room a group of fairly sophisticated writers were doing much the same thing — ignoring the leader and talking of Woods.

• Expecting unprecedented numbers of reporters and photographers to follow him in the first round, the USGA sent two of its staff onto the course to maintain control, a measure usually saved for the last-round leader.

• Woods lives in Orlando, Florida. The week before the Open he bought a sandwich at a Subway restaurant in a suburban

Caddie Mike "Fluff" Cowan had become a celebrity along with his boss.

This girl got even Tiger's attention.

mall. Visiting the mall later that day, one of his friends told him people were still talking about it.

• A 16-year-old girl from a high school bearing the nickname of Tigers showed up at Congressional wearing a tiger outfit borrowed from the school's band. She managed to wheedle an autograph from him.

All this for a 21-year-old golfer.

Woods, however, is an exceptional 21-year-old golfer. Submitting to questions by an assortment of reporters, Woods was asked little about golf. A few selections of what he was asked:

• Obviously black people want you to be black and Asians want you to be Asian. How do you address those people who want Tiger Woods to be them?

• With the frenzy that sort of follows you around, and crowds rushing to you when you get out of your car, and the letters you get from racists, do you ever

The largest galleries of the week trekked behind golf's new phenomenon.

fear for your safety?

• I wonder if you're concerned about the behavior of your galleries and if you feel it's time to say something to them before they become detrimental to the game?

• With so many people expecting you to win this tournament, are you beginning to feel the pressure?

• Can you describe what this last year has been like for you?

• With the Tigermania of the last nine months, a lot of your peers have said there are other golfers on the tour. Do you feel for them and what they're going through because of this Tiger-against-the-world attitude?

• Can you talk a little bit about what it's like to be a role model for so many young people?

• If you fail to win another major this year, would 1997 be a disappointment for you?

• Where are you staying?

He had all the right answers. A condensation of a few:

On his own racial make-up. He said that's just going to happen because it's the way of our society. Until everyone is classified not by race but as being part of the human race, everyone will classify another person.

On the frenzy of the crowds following him. He said he has received threatening letters as well as other things he didn't identify. "But, you know, that's just part of being a minority in a sport. It happens … It's just something that I've kind of dealt with …"

On the behavior of his galleries. He said he wished he could say something to them, "but if I would say something I might be looked at as a bad guy. You have to understand, these people are coming into the game; they don't know. It would be like me watching cricket."

On whether he feels pressure. He said

In the minds of his fans, Woods already was alongside such legends as Jack Nicklaus.

his parents taught him never to listen to other people's expectations of him. "You should live your own life and live up to your own expectations."

On his last year. He said his life had changed, that once he won the Masters Tournament he became more recognizable. "People are starting to recognize me when I go out in public. That's been the biggest adjustment."

On Tigermania and its effect on other players. He said he feels for those who play with him and in front of him because the galleries run ahead from his group and distract the players up ahead, "and after I putt out, sometimes the galleries start to move again. It's tough for guys who have to make a crucial par or birdie putt. Their concentration is interrupted."

On what it's like to be a role model. He said it's an honor, that he's in a position where he can help people in a positive way, and "what more do you want? I can influence kids in a good way. And I try; I try to do my best. I mean, that's perfect."

On whether he would consider 1997 a failure if he didn't win another important championship to add to the Masters, he said he would consider 1997 a great year whether he won or lost. "I've accomplished a lot of my goals already."

On where he was staying. He said, "In a room."

Cool. Very cool.

Opposite page, with all the Tigermania, you wouldn't have even known these guys were there.

Phil Mickelson was a 1997 victor at Bay Hill.

Mark O'Meara had posted two early year wins.

Steve Elkington was second on the money list.

Steve Jones returned as defending champion.

97th
U.S. Open
First Round

As the 97th United States Open Champion-ship began under overcast and threatening skies, no one quite knew what to expect of the Congressional Country Club course. It was no secret that it was long, but length doesn't mean much to the modern golfer of Open caliber. The rough was fierce and the greens speedy, but only a few in the field hadn't already played under those condi-tions. The germane question seemed to be if it would yield to superior golf. There was no precedent.

Ken Venturi had won the 1964 Open, Congressional's first, with 278, but Rees Jones had created a practically new course early in the 1990s. Tom Weiskopf had shot four rounds in the 60s in 1995 and won the Senior Open with 275 over the new course, but set up for the Open, the holes played longer, the rough stood higher, and the fairways pinched narrower.

One circumstance suggested Congres-sional might be ripe for low scoring. A rainy spring had soaked the ground. While it helped the rough grow straight and tall, more importantly it soaked the greens and made them easier to hold than the USGA had hoped. As a countermeasure, the club installed powerful fans that shot a stream of drying wind across every green for two solid weeks. As the championship devel-oped, Congressional did extremely well. It gave up strokes to superior ball-striking, and it claimed a difficult price from loose and indifferent golf and for flawed think-ing.

As early scores filtered in the first day, Congressional seemed to be holding up. It did, in fact, play tough; birdies won on the early holes were being snatched back on later holes. There was one exception: Colin

Montgomerie held on to what he took. With birdies on the seventh, ninth and 10th holes, he stood three under par with eight holes to play.

Others weren't doing so well. Chris Perry stood two under par after 13 holes but played the last five in two over for his 70; Loren Roberts had birdied the first two holes, then played the fourth, fifth and sixth in bogey-birdie-bogey, double-bogeyed the dangerous 10th, and shot 72; Nick Price shot 34 on the first nine but came back in 37 for his 71; and Jack Nicklaus had gone out in 34 as well, but he double-bogeyed the 11th and bogeyed the 13th and shot 73.

Others were having worse days. Greg Norman and Phil Mickelson went out in 39 and lost another stroke coming in. Both shot 75. Vijay Singh opened with a birdie, then bogeyed the next three holes and shot 71; Nick Faldo shot an erratic 72 with two double bogeys and never figured; and Curtis Strange went out in 38, double-bogeyed the 10th and shot 79.

The pattern continued through the day. At the end of the round only nine men had finished in the 60s and eight more had come in with 70. In a field of 156 of the best players in the game, only 17 managed par or better. Two years earlier, at Shinnecock Hills, which lies exposed to the winds on eastern Long Island, 10 men shot in the 60s and another 15 matched its par of 70.

Three of Congressional's holes had been especially troubling — the sixth and the 10th, both normally three-shot holes for Congressional's members, and the 16th, a

Colin Montgomerie said he was "very com-fortable" on Open courses because of his ac-curacy.

regulation 441-yard par-four. The sixth and 10th, which measured in order, 475 and 466 yards, had been shortened to bring the greens into range of well-played second shots and labeled par-fours. Shorn up by a stone wall, the sixth green sits beyond a wide pond, and another pond crowds the right side of the 10th green.

During the first day of play, the sixth claimed 15 double bogeys, the 16th 12, and the sixth 11.

When the day ended, Montgomerie had shot 65 and led the field by one stroke over Hal Sutton, who hadn't been heard from in years, and Steve Stricker, who has never reached his potential. They shot 66s. Tom Lehman, with 35-32, and Mark McNulty, with 37-30, stood another stroke back at 67. Hideki Kase, a 38-year-old Japanese who had qualified by shooting 138 at the Woodmont Country Club, another Washington-area club, shot 68, along with Dave Schreyer. Jeff Sluman and Justin Leonard shot 69s.

Meantime, Ernie Els shot 71, Jeff Maggert 73, and Tiger Woods a maddening 74 that upset him terribly.

Montgomerie's 65 stood out like a beacon. While it had been matched by T.C. Chen in 1985, only Jack Nicklaus and Tom Weiskopf, with 63s in 1980, and Lee Mackey, with 64 in 1950, have opened with lower scores. It could have been even lower, because he had legitimate birdie openings on nearly every hole. One of the early starters, off the first tee at 8 o'clock, grouped with Davis Love III and Phil Mickelson, he shaved two strokes from par on the first nine, then raced back in 32.

The formula for playing any Open course is simple: hit the fairways and hit the greens. Montgomerie followed directions almost perfectly. Even though he is possibly the straightest driver of all the leading players, Monty left the driver in his bag and used his three wood from the tee. He was deadly. He hit 13 of the 14 fairways on driving holes, and 16 of the 18 greens. Only

Opposite, Tom Lehman, after his 67, waved to the crowd.

Hal Sutton shot 66 with no bogeys.

Steve Stricker (66) had four birdies in a row.

Mark McNulty (67) shot 30 on the second nine.

Dave Schreyer (68) just won a Hooters event.

First Round

Colin Montgomerie	65	-5
Hal Sutton	66	-4
Steve Stricker	66	-4
Mark McNulty	67	-3
Tom Lehman	67	-3
Hideki Kase	68	-2
Dave Schreyer	68	-2
Jeff Sluman	69	-1
Justin Leonard	69	-1

one missed green cost him a stroke. His approach to the wonderful 17th hole, a downhill par-four of 480 yards, caught the right greenside bunker and he bogeyed. Ironically, the other missed green saved his round.

Montgomerie had begun with an annoying string of botched birdie openings. After some sparkling approaches, he missed from eight, six and four feet on the first three holes, and looked as if this would not be his day when he pulled his tee shot into the left rough on the intimidating sixth hole. An experienced player, Montgomerie recognized futility when he saw it; standing ankle-deep in the wiry, unyielding grass with no hope of reaching the green, he chopped his ball back into play, then lofted a stunning eight iron that nearly knocked the flagstick from the hole. His ball braked little more than a foot from the hole and he saved his par four.

That was all he needed; over the next 12 holes he ran off six birdies and lost only the stroke at the 17th.

The sixth was the key. Montgomerie called it "the most important par I've made for a long time. It was the most vital hole of the day. If I had missed that par at the sixth, if I had made five, which was in the cards, I probably wouldn't have birdied the seventh and therefore not the ninth, 10th and 11th. That par enabled me to hit a good shot into the seventh," a 174-yard par-three.

Four under after the 11th, Monty went to six under with two superb irons to four

Jeff Sluman (69) bogeyed two of the last three.

Justin Leonard (69) hit 15 greens in regulation.

feet on both the 13th and 16th. Then he lost the stroke at the 17th, where he missed from 15 feet, and settled for his 65.

It was a round that impressed even Montgomerie himself.

"My distance control with my irons was as good as I've ever seen it," he said, then explained, "If I had 158 yards to the pin, I would hit it 158 yards. If I had 178, I would hit it 178."

Montgomerie finished a few minutes after 1 o'clock. By then Woods had been out for an hour, getting nowhere. As the 1996 United States Amateur champion, he was grouped with Steve Jones, the Open champion, and Tom Lehman, the British Open champion. Naturally he carried such a big gallery it made Montgomerie's seem little more than friends and acquaintances.

All three walked onto the first tee close behind one another, with Woods last. In a moment of levity after the crowd's cheers died down, Jones claimed the ovation for himself and, facing the grandstands urged the gallery, "Now let's hear it for Tiger Woods." It loosened everyone.

Hideki Kase (68) made four birdies.

Tiger Woods tumbled to 74. He said, "I hit some bad shots and didn't make the putts I needed."

Woods began as if he might play as well at Congressional as he had at Augusta, when he won the Masters by 12 strokes. He gave himself birdie chances on the first two holes — his putt on the first actually hit the cup — but he birdied only the second, a long par-three of 235 yards, by rifling a two-iron shot little more than two feet from the hole. Then he slipped on the third, three-putting for a bogey five from the back of the green.

But he birdied the fourth to go back to one under par, quickly lost the stroke again by three-putting the fifth, then misjudged his distance once again on the sixth, leaving his ball lying against the high rough at the back of the green. With his marvelous short game, Woods took his club almost straight up, dropped it down behind the ball and ran it within easy holing distance for his par. Even par then, Woods played another stunning tee shot into the seventh no more than two or three feet from the cup.

Out in 34, one under a difficult par, Woods was in good position to make a run at Montgomerie. He birdied the 10th, Congressional's second most difficult hole, then

began to unravel.

Although it isn't easy, the 11th measures just 415 yards and the flagstick was located toward the green's back left, two-thirds of the way back and perhaps 25 feet from the left edge, not a difficult position. Woods went for it but misjudged again, flew his ball over the green and into the trees, pitched over the green again, and made six. He had lost both strokes he had taken from Congressional.

Now his inexperience began showing. After a routine par three on the 12th, he jerked his drive on the 13th into the rough and tried to play an iron to the green. It can't be done. His shot ran no more than halfway and he bogeyed again.

This was the beginning of a series of strange drives. He went from the left rough on the 13th to the right rough on the 14th, and back to the left rough on the 15th. He escaped with par only on the 14th — no one will ever know why his putt didn't drop. As he had on the 13th, Woods had thrown away a stroke on the 15th by playing a foolish shot. As Woods tried for distance from that deep and treacherous rough, the grass tore the club from his hands. The

Spectators found a good view on the sixth.

ball flew across the fairway and into the right rough.

His frustration broke through again on the 16th. When he overshot the green he cried, "You're kidding me."

He made his par there and again on the 17th, but then he paid the price for his impatience on the 18th, the par-three across a lake. Up first, Lehman had played a nice little draw that almost went into the hole on the fly. Whether Woods tried to copy Lehman's shot is unknown, but he started his shot left of the flag and watched it curl farther left, catch the steep bank, and tumble into the water. It was his second double bogey of the second nine. After going out in 34, he had come back in 40 and shot 74.

When his ball sank under the water, Woods turned away, and with his face glaring in anger, slammed his club into his bag. Obviously his golf had disturbed him.

It seemed to have no effect on Lehman. He very quietly birdied four holes on the home nine, shot 67, picked up nearly a stroke a hole on Woods with his closing 32, and placed himself in position to challenge for the lead.

Hale Irwin (70) took a drop beside his reflection.

After Colin Montgomerie's virtuoso 65 in the first round, Phil Mickelson, a witness to every shot, said it was the finest example of ball-striking he had ever seen. Watching him hit one fairway after another, Ben Crenshaw exclaimed, "My God, he's so straight!" and Montgomerie himself said, "This is possibly the best round of golf I've ever put together in major golf."

At the same time Tiger Woods said very little, and no one praised his game, since he had fallen nine strokes behind Montgomerie with his 74.

Montgomerie had been a model of sound, Open-style golf that first day, hitting fairways and hitting greens. Woods, though, had stumbled through the second nine, where he had hit just four fairways and four greens.

Something happened overnight. Playing the loosest kind of golf, missing more fairways and greens than he hit, grumbling about the humidity and the galleries, and complaining of a headache, Monty slipped to 76 and fell behind, while Woods regained his poise, smiled more than he scowled, played the level of golf he had shown at Augusta, shot 67, and climbed from a tie for 80th place into a tie for ninth.

While those two exchanged roles, Tom Lehman quietly shot an even-par 70 and moved into first place at 137. Both Stewart Cink, a tall, 24-year-old former Nike Tour player, and Ernie Els, the 1994 champion, thrust themselves into the chase by shooting 67s and climbing into second place, one stroke behind, and Jeff Maggert, who had tied for fourth at Shinnecock Hills two years earlier, slipped into a tie for fourth place at 139 after shooting 66.

Meantime, Hal Sutton went from 66 to 73, Mark McNulty went from 67 to 73 as well, and Steve Stricker slipped from 66 to 76.

It was an eventful day. Not only did the lead change hands, but the round couldn't be completed until Saturday morning because of a two-hour lightning delay. When daylight ran out at 8:32 p.m. and play was called off for the day, the round had taken 13 and a half hours, and it still wasn't finished.

Then there was John Daly's latest episode. Before the lightning scare and after going out in 38, Daly walked off the course without saying anything, leaving Els and Payne Stewart, whom he was with, along with his caddie waiting on the 10th tee. They finished without him.

The interruptions came at a time when the players were taking the measure of Congressional, as trying an Open course as anyone could remember. Where only eight men had matched or bettered par in the opening round, 20 men shot in the 60s in the second, and five others shot 70.

Maggert's was the lowest score of this difficult day. Rain had fallen briefly in the early morning, then returned just before lunchtime. Sirens screamed when weathermen detected lightning in the neighborhood, leading the USGA to suspended play a few minutes before noon. The pause put a strain on the schedule. This was the day of the 36-hole cut, when the field would be pared to the low 60 scores and anyone within 10 strokes of the leader, but when play resumed just after 2 o'clock, it was obvious the entire field could not complete

"My chances must be quite good now," said Ernie Els after his 67 for 138.

Tom Lehman (137) took the lead by one.

Stewart Cink (138) said he putted well.

Jeff Maggert (139) went from 73 to 66.

David Ogrin (139) had rounds of 70, 69.

Mark McNulty (140) went from 67 to 73.

Hal Sutton (139) also shot 73.

36 holes. The day's play ended with 45 men still on the course; they would finish at 7 o'clock Saturday morning.

The delay caught even Lehman, Woods and Steve Jones, who had begun at 7:40 in the morning. The siren blew just as Lehman teed his ball on the 17th hole. By then he stood one under par and had played extraordinarily sound golf. Over 16 holes he had missed just two fairways and two greens. After a somewhat rocky start — he three-putted the second and missed both the fairway and green of the third, losing a total of two strokes — Lehman settled down, and playing some first-class irons, birdied three of the next six holes on the first nine and went out in 34. Starting back he three-putted again at the 10th, then nearly holed his pitch at the 14th, setting up his last birdie of the day.

Something seemed to be missing when play began after the rainstorm passed. Neither Lehman, Woods nor Jones looked sharp. Lehman missed both the fairway and the green of the 17th but still scraped out his par, Woods three-putted from 35 feet for a bogey five, and Jones made seven. Then Lehman missed the 18th green and bogeyed, ending his day with an even-par round and the Open lead.

Once again Woods had captured much of the attention, but unlike the opening round, he rewarded his galleries with first-class golf. Sticking to his plan to use his driver only occasionally and relying on his two iron and three wood, Woods missed only the 13th and 17th fairways. While both of them cost him bogeys, he had the round under control by then.

He began by birdieing four of the first seven holes, mainly through deadly iron play that left him little to do on the greens. For example, he hit an eight iron to six feet on the first, a six iron to eight feet at the third, another eight iron to three feet at the fifth, and a seven iron to four feet at the seventh. Four under par then, he turned in 31 and played the first three holes of the home nine in par, two strokes better than he had in the first round.

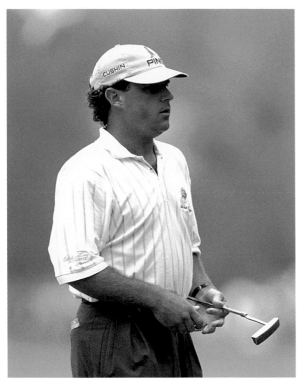

Kelly Gibson (141) had 10 birdies in two days.

Tiger Woods (141) got four early birdies.

Second Round

Tom Lehman	67 - 70 – 137	-3
Ernie Els	71 - 67 – 138	-2
Stewart Cink	71 - 67 – 138	-2
Jeff Maggert	73 - 66 – 139	-1
David Ogrin	70 - 69 – 139	-1
Hal Sutton	66 - 73 – 139	-1
Scott Hoch	71 - 68 – 139	-1
Mark McNulty	67 - 73 – 140	E

Still four under par, Woods gave one stroke away at the 13th by pushing his two-iron tee shot into the rough and missing the green, but then he birdied the 14th with another beautifully played seven iron to 12 feet. Then he inspired rousing cheers with two Brobdingnagian shots on the 583-yard 15th — a driver and three wood to the back of the green. He birdied, of course, his seventh of the day. Five under par now, on his way to 65 if he could play the next three holes in par.

He wouldn't make it. He lost a stroke on the 16th just before the sirens called a halt. Then he bogeyed the 17th and climbed the long hill to the 18th tee where on Thursday he had pulled his tee shot into the lake.

He nearly did it again. With the flagstick in the front right corner, about 15 feet from the front and 15 feet from the side, Woods played his eight iron. As his ball flew toward the green the wind swirled into his face and he cried, "Oh, no. It could end up short." It did indeed, but the wet grass held the ball up and he saved his par three and the 67.

Montgomerie, meantime, wasn't the glorious player he had been the previous day. He was having all sorts of problems, not only with his golf but with his temperament as well. Red-haired, red-faced and rather pudgy, he had never stood up in the heat and humidity of an American summer. His caddie said that every time Monty bent over to putt, he felt faint. Once he

Scott Dunlap (141) birdied six of the first 13.

walked to the gallery ropes and asked his wife, Eimear, if she could find a first-aid station.

The gallery upset him most. Unruly and loud, some spectators heckled him and some cheered when he missed a putt. He became upset even when someone called for him to "Shake it off." Meant to encourage him, it enraged him instead. Finally, when someone screamed, "You da man," as Phil Mickelson played a drive, Montgomerie, his face by now a glowing crimson, erupted.

"Hey, hey," he yelled, walking toward the gallery ropes.

Confronted by Montgomerie's glowering anger, the man said, "Sorry about that."

Not appeased easily, Monty shot back, "No you're not. You're not sorry at all."

Then he drove into the rough once again and made yet another bogey, his fifth of the day. Another on the 17th moved him to six over par for the day, and he struggled to save his three on the 18th after missing the green.

Colin Montgomerie (141) tested his patience.

Jack Nicklaus, Ben Crenshaw and Hale Irwin all made the 36-hole cut.

After signing his scorecard, he seemed calm enough, and he even talked about his position, which had gone from five under par to one over.

"I didn't play well," he said. "I've got to regroup and try to find what I was doing Thursday," when he played such precise golf. "If I do, I can still win. I know I'm capable of scoring low on this course. I love this course. I think it's a great golf course."

That may be, but Congressional held no charm for Daly. Without saying anything to anybody — not even his caddie — he slipped into the clubhouse on his way from the ninth green to the 10th tee without anyone's noticing, changed his shoes, climbed into his car, and drove off. Els and Stewart and all three caddies waited for him. After perhaps 10 minutes, a USGA Rules official told the group to play on.

Daly was playing in his third tournament since an eight-week program at the Betty Ford Center in Rancho Mirage, Cali-

Joel Kribel (148), retrieving his golf ball here at No. 10, was low amateur despite missing the cut.

Greg Norman (154) missed the cut by seven.

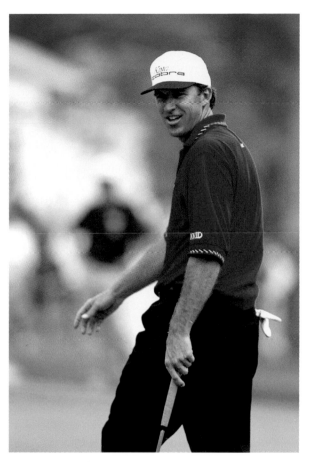

Steve Jones (147) was on the cut score.

fornia. A statement obviously prepared by the public relations department of the Callaway golf club company, which signed him recently, quoted him as saying, "Even though I thought I was going to be strong enough to come right back and play three straight weeks, I found out I was wrong. I just started feeling real weak after a few holes, and by the time I got to the ninth, I was just physically exhausted."

Daly's withdrawal dropped the field to 155. When the end finally came the following morning, 84 players had shot 147 or better and survived for the last two rounds.

Jack Nicklaus was among them. After his opening 73, he came back with 71 and, at 144, climbed into a tie for 36th place, along with Tom Kite, the 1992 champion; Stewart, who had won in 1991; Paul Azinger, the 1993 PGA champion; and Larry Mize, who had won the 1987 Masters.

While Nicklaus made it into the final 36 holes, his son Gary didn't. With 77, he shot 150, three strokes over the cut.

Nor did Greg Norman make it. His mind more on his father, who had had heart surgery in Australia, than on his golf, Greg went from 75 to 79, and for the first time missed the cut in both the Open and the Masters. Ian Woosnam missed as well, after winning the Volvo PGA Championship in Europe a month or so earlier, along with Corey Pavin, the 1995 champion; Bernhard Langer, usually a reliable player who had won the Masters twice; Mark Brooks, the current PGA champion; Curtis Strange, the last to win successive Opens; and Steve Hart, who had been called early Thursday morning to fill a spot left open by the withdrawal of Costantino Rocca, the Italian golfer Daly had beaten in a playoff for the 1995 British Open.

For a time on Saturday the galleries wondered not about who would win but when, if ever, the Open would end. After another thunderstorm set back the schedule more than two hours once again, the gloomy ones predicted that with luck we could have a champion by the following Wednesday. The storm had dumped more than half an inch of rain on already wet grounds, and forced 21 players to come back Sunday morning to finish what they had begun Saturday afternoon.

The day had not begun pleasantly, then menacing black clouds had formed throughout the afternoon. With the threat of lightning, danger warnings went up on the scoreboards, and sirens sounded a little after 5 o'clock. Within a few minutes the rain gushed down, turning a few holes into bogs, the club's paved roads and parking lots into rivers, and soaking the 30,000 spectators, who squeezed into food and merchandise tents for shelter.

The round resumed a little after 7 o'clock, but with so little daylight left, even a field of 84 couldn't complete the round. When the light grew dim, at 8:20 p.m., the USGA suspended play; those left on the course would return Sunday morning, play their few holes, then wait for their afternoon starting times.

This was another bewildering day when no one could be certain who held command. Maggert held first place at the rain delay and when play was suspended overnight, and Lehman led through 54 holes. Els moved into a tie with Maggert with a string of three birdies Sunday morning.

Tom Lehman (205) picked up three strokes on Sunday morning to lead by two.

When the round ended, Lehman led with 205, five under par, two strokes ahead of Maggert and Els, at 207, and Montgomerie stood at 208. No one else had broken par. Hal Sutton dropped behind with another 73, Mark McNulty had sunk deeper with 75, and Tiger Woods could do nothing, in spite of a dedicated and loyal following who urged him to play as they knew he could. Beginning the round at one over par, he lost three more strokes and shot 73. With 214 for 54 holes, he would play no further part in the championship.

Meantime, the quality of the golf improved over what it had been. At the end of the round, 16 men had broken par 70 and five others had matched it. Nine of the 11 men at 211 or better had shot in the 60s.

Montgomerie played the best golf. Recovering from his grim 76 of the second round, he shot 67, which left him three strokes behind Lehman. Maggert might have done better, but after shooting another 31 on the first nine, he came back in 37 and shot 68. Els made a substantial move Sunday morning by finishing 4-3-3-3 — three birdies and a par — and shooting 69.

With the second round's overnight delay and the need to regroup the players, the third round didn't begin until 10:10 a.m., much later than the usual time. Because of the late start, the field had to be grouped in threes rather than the customary pairs. As the 36-hole leader, Lehman went off last with Els and Stewart Cink, just behind Maggert, Sutton and David Ogrin.

Lehman moved quickly from three under par to five under with exceptional irons that left him only short putts for birdies on both the fourth and fifth holes. Leading now, he drove into the heavy rough on the

Ernie Els (207) was two over on Saturday.

demanding sixth, played safely back to the fairway, then nearly saved par with a pitch to five feet. The putt missed; back to four under for 42 holes, one under for the round.

He recovered the lost stroke by birdieing the seventh with another blistering shot to six feet, eased past the eighth, the easiest par-four at Congressional, then pushed his drive into the right rough on the ninth, a long and hard par-five of 607 yards.

It is an unwise man who takes risks from this demonic rough. The experienced player will swallow hard and chop his ball back into play, then move on. Lehman again chose the prudent pitch to the fairway, but now he stood miles away with a one iron for his third shot. Then the sirens called, and Lehman ducked into the clubhouse to think it over.

While Lehman and the others reflected on what they might expect when the round resumed, the grounds crew worked at warp speed to make Congressional playable. Men

Opposite, Jeff Maggert (207) led before the rain delay on Saturday afternoon.

Colin Montgomerie (208) recovered with 67.

Jay Haas (210) had fought back to even par after his three-over start.

with squeegees swooshed water off the greens and fairways, while bucket-wielding crews bailed out bunkers and rebuilt their washed-out faces, as still others carrying portable blowers whooshed away debris. When play began again after 7 p.m., the course was certainly playable but terribly difficult. Balls plugged in bunkers, and the rough, already pitiless, had become savage with the rain. One good thing: the rain had softened the greens.

Maggert, meantime, had found the combination to Congressional's first nine. He had gone out in 31 in the second round and now shot another in the third round. After birdieing both the eighth and ninth, he had gone to the 10th and driven 25 yards past Sutton and Ogrin, the other two in his group. That was as far as he could go before the USGA stopped play.

Montgomerie, meanwhile, had found his game and was off to an even better start than his first round. He had gone out in 33 then, but now he shot 31, two strokes bet-

Third Round

Tom Lehman	67 - 70 - 68 – 205	-5
Jeff Maggert	73 - 66 - 68 – 207	-3
Ernie Els	71 - 67 - 69 – 207	-3
Colin Montgomerie	65 - 76 - 67 – 208	-2
Jay Haas	73 - 69 - 68 – 210	E
Tommy Tolles	74 - 67 - 69 – 210	E
David Ogrin	70 - 69 - 71 – 210	E

ter. Where he had birdied only two holes Thursday, he had birdied four on Saturday, one of them that will be remembered by everyone who saw it.

After a nice tee shot into the seventh had placed him about 20 feet from the hole, Monty faced a perplexing downhill putt with a serious break. After studying the line

Billy Andrade (211) took a chunk of U.S. Open rough with this shot (opposite).

Scott Hoch (211) was among those with an outside chance to win entering the last round.

Tommy Tolles (210) had started with 74.

for some time, he lined up to start the ball perhaps 20 feet or more left of the hole. Then he backed off, grinned a little at the absurdity of it, realigned himself, and laid a gentle tap against the ball. It ghosted down the slope, took the break just as Montgomerie had figured it would, and dropped into the cup. When the putt fell, Monty dropped his putter, turned to the gallery and held out his hands, obviously astonished.

Just as the saving par on the sixth had sparked his first round, the birdie here seemed to give him life. He made a three on the eighth and a four on the ninth, two more birdies. Three under for 45 holes now, Montgomerie began the long slog home by bogeying the 10th. Back to two under.

The rain interrupted his round on the 12th, which frustrated him enough, but then, soaked with perspiration, he tried to buy a new shirt in the golf shop but couldn't find his size. More unhappiness.

While Montgomerie had been climbing

back into the race by stages, Sutton had done it all at once. One under par when the day began, he played the first seven holes with one birdie and a bogey, then came to the eighth, at 362 yards the shortest of the par-fours. After a nicely placed drive left of center-fairway, where it curves to the right, he had just a pitching wedge to the green, nearly encircled by bunkers. Sutton played the shot just right; it carried past the hole, set in the front left corner, took the vicious backspin, and drew back into the cup for an eagle two. Now Sutton stood three under par, tied with Cink, within reach of the lead.

When the suspension ended and the players were called back to the course, they walked into a surreal scene. Congressional lay under a wispy fog. It was eerie. Unconnected voices could be heard through the mist, but the milky fog blocked the view. It was strangely difficult for the players; they could see a shot start off, but they couldn't follow its flight. Lehman said later, "the haze was so heavy I didn't see a single shot I hit."

David Ogrin (210) holed out on No. 2.

Olin Browne (211) had a third-round 69.

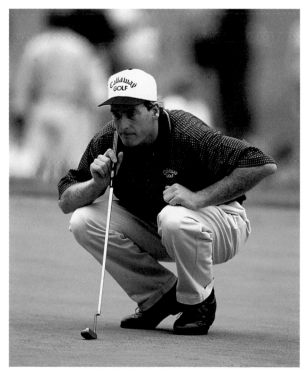

Jim Furyk (211) was also in contention.

A fierce storm swept through Congressional just after 5 p.m., forcing a postponement.

Three birdies and a par on Sunday morning brought Els (207) within two strokes of the lead.

Perhaps not, but he saw the ninth green well enough to drill his one iron into the rough short of the green, then chop it out and save his par five. He and Maggert were tied at five under par, but while Maggert ran off three pars, Lehman botched the 10th and 11th and dropped two strokes behind. Maggert gave one stroke away at the 13th, and when play ended for the day Maggert held first place at four under, Lehman stood three under, Montgomerie two under, and Els even par, tied with Ogrin and Jay Haas for seventh place.

Lehman said the golf course played two clubs longer following the rain.

"It played so long," he said, "and the rough was so heavy." And he wasn't quite sure how to handle the fog, so "I just hit it and it disappeared into the mist."

The fog had flown by the next morning, along with Maggert's lead. He began with pars on the 15th and 16th, but he pushed his approach to the 17th into the deep rough and bogeyed, and with a chance to win it back on the 18th, groaned when his 10-foot birdie putt caught the lip of the hole but wouldn't fall.

On the other hand, Montgomerie did indeed hole from 25 feet or so for a birdie two on the 18th, and Sutton, once so close, doomed himself when his tee shot skidded off the left side of the green and into the water.

Lehman, meantime, birdied the 14th with a marvelous pitch less than a yard from the hole, and finished with a nice draw to about seven feet on the 18th. The putt fell. With the birdie he had picked up three strokes on Maggert over those last five holes and climbed into first place once again.

For once the skies over Congressional were free from the threat of rain. The sun had burned away the overcast and only a few white clouds drifted in a light breeze as the spectators began streaming through the gates and the early groups teed off for the final round of the 97th Open.

Off among the early starters, Jack Nicklaus drew a good crowd as he completed his 41st Open. He shot 74, and with 293 for the 72 holes, tied for 52nd place. At 57 he was probably the oldest man who ever played 72 holes in the Open, and statisticians told us that on the weekend he played his 10,000th hole in major competition.

Tiger Woods drew his usual sizable following as well, but most spectators either hung around to follow the last two groups or found space near strategic points, many of them lining the hillsides overlooking the two closing holes.

President Clinton and his daughter, Chelsea, found positions just as good. Arriving later in the day, they watched for a while from a tower behind the 16th green, then moved on to the television facility by the 17th and 18th. As far as anyone knows, Mr. Clinton is the first sitting President to have seen an Open since 1921, when Warren G. Harding presented the trophy to Jim Barnes at Columbia Country Club, a few miles away in Chevy Chase, another suburb of Washington.

Those who chose to walk with the leaders had let themselves in for a session of day-long tension watching Ernie Els, Colin Montgomerie, Tom Lehman and Jeff Maggert play their hearts out over an unforgiv-

Ernie Els' iron play would be crucial in the fourth round.

ing course that tolerated no loose shots.

While Lehman began the day two strokes ahead, he bogeyed two of the first four holes, and then they were never more than two strokes apart until the very end. Indeed, they spent most of the round either tied or within a stroke of one another as they battled stroke-for-stroke over this long, unmerciful golf course. As late as the 11th hole they were still tied, each man at four under par. Not one of them yielded until the very end when Els played superbly under intense pressure. By then the championship had become a test not only of who among them had the golf skill, but of who had the nerve, the control and the strength of will to play the shots he needed with so much at stake.

In the end, the championship came down to the 17th hole, where every other championship at Congressional had finished since Ken Venturi won the 1964 Open. It was the key; it ruined both Montgomerie and Lehman — Maggert had fallen back on the 13th — and it showed that even when his heart must have been racing, Els could still play the shot he had to play, a stunning five iron drawn toward the dangerous hole position on the green's back left corner, where it juts into the lake.

With that shot, Els had hit every green since overshooting the 13th, while Montgomerie and Maggert had missed two and Lehman one. Tom would miss one more, though, one that cost him a heavy price. Els had the steadier nerves, especially with that shot into the green. It brought cheers from the gallery and gasps from those who understood the difficulty of it and the precision in pulling it off.

While Els played the shot he needed,

43

The following leaderboard is shown:

LEADERS	TODAY	HOLE	TOTAL
LEHMAN	0	2	5
MAGGERT	0	2	5
ELS	1	3	3
MONTGOMERIE	0	3	3
TOLLES	2	3	0
HAAS	1	3	2
GRIN	1	4	1
KOCH	1	4	
FURYK	0	4	1
TWAY		4	5

	TODAY	THRU 2		TOTAL
O MAGGERT				3
O LEHMAN				5

Tom Lehman (278) led by two strokes until making bogeys on the third and fourth holes.

Jay Haas (282) was pleased by a top-10 finish.

Tommy Tolles (282) dropped back with 72.

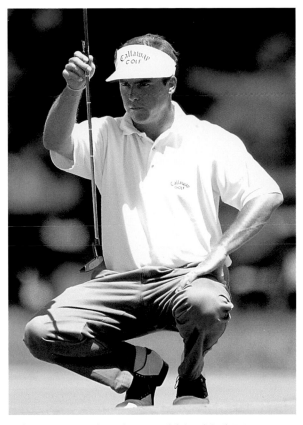

Olin Browne (282) posted his third 71.

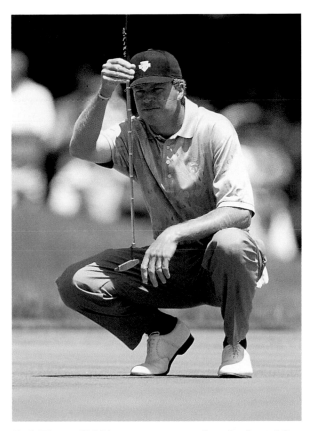

Bob Tway (282) was even par for the last 36.

Montgomerie hit into the rough on the bank of a greenside bunker miles away, and Lehman, one stroke behind by then, hit his approach just a touch fat and into the lake. Now Els had the Open in hand.

These four made up an interesting combination. Els, Lehman and Montgomerie had either won the Open or at least threatened to win it, while Maggert had never placed higher than fourth, in 1995 at Shinnecock Hills, another severe course that asked for everyone's best golf.

Montgomerie and Lehman had suffered most. This was the third consecutive year Lehman had held either the lead or a share of it after 54 holes, and yet he hadn't won. He had slipped to 74 in the last round of the 1995 championship and dropped to third place, and he had been unlucky in 1996. Tied with Steve Jones playing the last hole, he drove into a fairway bunker and bogeyed. Jones made his par and beat Lehman by one stroke.

Montgomerie had come close in 1992 and again in 1994. An early starter in 1992, he finished with 288, which looked good at the time, but Jeff Sluman came along later and shot 287, and then Tom Kite won it with 285. Two years later Monty tied with Els and Loren Roberts at Oakmont, but he played terrible golf through the early holes of the playoff. He shot 78 and simply didn't figure.

Els, of course, had won three years earlier, but he had missed the cut the following year and tied for fifth in 1996. Nevertheless, he had been one of those golfers whose power and easy rhythm had marked him from the first as a player of fascinating potential. While it is true he had blundered through the finish at Oakmont and played two horrible holes at the start of the playoff, he did eventually win. Still it was a little surprising to find him in position to win at Congressional after he had played such indifferent golf through

45

Els hit about five yards short of the 10th green, then holed his pitch shot to tie for the lead.

most of the season and had missed the cut at Avenel the previous week.

Nevertheless, he had boosted himself into the chase with three early-morning birdies winding up his third round, and now he had his chance to add another U.S. Open. At three under par, Els was paired with Montgomerie, one stroke behind him, in the next-to-last group, just ahead of Lehman, the leader at five under, and Maggert, tied with Els.

While Els played steady, par golf through the early holes, Montgomerie caught him with a nice nine iron to four feet on the first and Lehman bungled both the third and fourth, driving in the rough left of the third fairway for the fourth consecutive day and then missing the fourth green with a seven iron. With those bogeys, Lehman slipped to three under par, tied with Els and Montgomerie, and for the first time Maggert led at four under. Maggert and Els had played nothing but pars so far, which was good enough on a course that made

Fourth Round

Ernie Els	71 - 67 - 69 - 69 – 276	-4
Colin Montgomerie	65 - 76 - 67 - 69 – 277	-3
Tom Lehman	67 - 70 - 68 - 73 – 278	-2
Jeff Maggert	73 - 66 - 68 - 74 – 281	+1
Bob Tway	71 - 71 - 70 - 70 – 282	+2
Olin Browne	71 - 71 - 69 - 71 – 282	+2
Jim Furyk	74 - 68 - 69 - 71 – 282	+2
Tommy Tolles	74 - 67 - 69 - 72 – 282	+2
Jay Haas	73 - 69 - 68 - 72 – 282	+2

par a standard of excellence.

When both Montgomerie and Els birdied the seventh, the 174-yard par-three, all three were tied at three under. In making his birdie, Els holed from around 20 feet, the longest putt any of them made all day. Right away Montgomerie holed on top of him from 10 feet.

Jim Furyk (282) said he had scrambled well in shooting a final-round 71.

Jeff Maggert's hopes were finally erased when he bogeyed No. 16. He took fourth place (281).

Scott Hoch (283) closed with 72-72.

David Ogrin (283) had a final 73.

The standing changed throughout the day. Maggert, Lehman and Montgomerie were tied at four under after the ninth, and then Els played a shot that gave him the boost he needed. The 10th hole is very hard. It measures 466 yards and its green lies alongside a pond. Since the ground in the fairway tilts slightly toward the water, the ball is more likely to fade than draw. With 180 yards to the flagstick, Els played a six iron that didn't have enough steam. It dropped maybe five yards short and stuck there. In trouble now, he took a lofted club, pitched it to the front of the green, and ran it into the hole. A birdie; now all four men were tied at four under par.

The birdie was especially important since Els had butchered the ninth, a long par-five, and made six while Montgomerie birdied.

They had been playing one great shot after another. Montgomerie had pitched within six feet and birdied the ninth. Lehman followed with a 180-yard six iron onto the 10th and then an even better pitch to four feet on the 11th, where the flagstick was tucked behind a bunker on the front right. Maggert covered the flag with a five

iron to the 12th, the par-three, after Els had played his five iron to 10 feet; then Lehman nearly holed a sand-wedge third shot on the 15th. Aside from Montgomerie's on the ninth, only two of those shots won birdies. Els made his two on the 12th and Lehman his four on the 15th.

Lehman had actually been putting erratically. He seemed to have pushed his putts on both the 10th and 11th and paid for it later.

Els had broken ahead with his birdie on the 12th, but he bogeyed the 13th, and once again all four were tied when Maggert dropped behind by three-putting the 13th. He was finished. He fell out for good with another bogey on the 16th, where he drove into the left rough and gambled on playing a three wood out. The ball carried over the green and under a grandstand. Now he stood two under with two to play, and only three men were left.

Lehman had bogeyed the 16th as well by missing the green with another seven iron. Now Els and Montgomerie stood on top at four under and Lehman had fallen back to three under.

Colin Montgomerie (277) discusses strategy with his caddie on the 12th tee.

The 18th hole gallery's proximity to the 17th caused Montgomerie to wait twice.

Lehman thought he had his shot at No. 17, but "caught it just a smidge on the heavy side" ...

Lehman still had hope, because both Els and Montgomerie had the 17th ahead of them. For all its perils — 480 downhill yards to a cape green with water left and behind, a nest of bunkers on the right, bordered by more of that punishing rough — it seemed to be no problem for Els. He smashed a three wood far down the fairway, then a 212-yard five iron about as well as it could have been played. It shot off straight, took a gentle turn to the left, cleared the trouble, and nestled on the back of the green within 15 feet of the hole. It joins the ranks of spectacular shots hit on crucial holes at the Open.

Meanwhile, Montgomerie, facing the same problems, left his approach out to the right and winced when it settled in the heavy grass. He would have to struggle to save his par.

Now Monty grew agitated and paced back and forth while everyone waited for him to play his next shot. He was upset because of the noise coming from the big gallery watching Jay Haas and Tommy Tolles hole out on the 18th green, just across

the lake from the 17th, and he didn't want to play such an important shot until they had settled down.

Montgomerie eventually played a nice pitch to about five feet and Els rolled his putt just past the cup. Then Montgomerie waited again, until Haas and Tolles had left the green and begun their climb to the clubhouse. Asked why he waited so long, he explained, "I didn't want to rush the most important putt I've ever hit."

After the 18th cleared, he stepped up to his ball and tapped it just right. It ran toward the hole, broke left and looked as if it would hit dead center. Suddenly it straightened out and rolled past. A bogey five. Montgomerie stared at it with some despair, but it was all over. Els holed his second putt and they moved on to the 18th with Els clutching a fragile lead.

Because of the delay, Lehman had seen everything from back up the 17th fairway. He knew he needed a birdie, but he also knew he would seldom have a better chance. He had ripped a driver into just the right position, less than 190 yards to

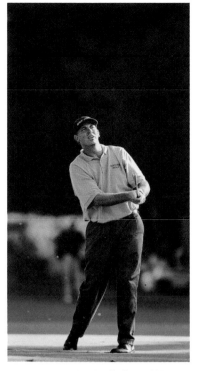
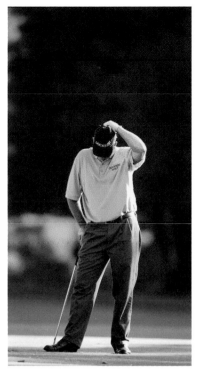
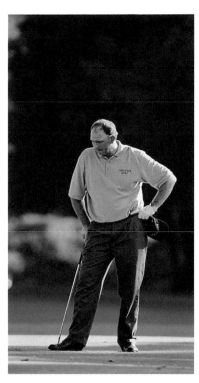

... seeing the ball fly off line, Lehman said "Oh, no," then was left only with his disappointment.

the hole, and he had just the right shot in mind — a slight right-to-left draw with a seven iron. It was the perfect shot for him, he said.

It didn't work. As soon as he hit it he knew he had lost the Open. Caught a little heavy, the ball curled too far left, hit the bank beside the green, and dived into the water.

As he saw the ball fly off line, Lehman moaned, "Oh, no," then covered his head with his hand and stood still as a statue. When after endless minutes Lehman moved again and took off his cap, his face wore a doleful expression, as if that one mis-played shot had torn the heart from him. He had been so close these last three years, and yet hadn't won. He even wondered if he was missing something inside.

Montgomerie wondered about himself as well, but he had been Europe's leading player four consecutive years, and disappointed though he was, he promised he would be back in 1998 for another try for what he called, "The world championship of golf."

Els celebrated his second U.S. Open victory.

A week after winning the Open, Ernie Els shot 64-68-67-69–268 at the Westchester Country Club, near New York, led every round for the second consecutive year, won the Buick Classic by two strokes over Jeff Maggert, and bolted to the top of the World Ranking. His sudden rise raised questions. Was he as good as he would ever be, or could he become even better? Fascinating questions.

Since he first made himself known, Els has been something of an enigma. Take 1997, for example. He played especially well in Europe, winning the Johnnie Walker Classic and placing second in the Volvo PGA, and he had won the Open championship of South Africa, his native land. But when he played in the United States he didn't perform as well. In his best finish he placed ninth at Greensboro, but of the 11 tournaments he played, he missed the cut in four. Then he suddenly won the national championship for the second time.

He had had other chances to win important tournaments, but his game had collapsed occasionally and he had tossed them away. He held the 1995 PGA Championship in his grip, three strokes ahead with 18 holes to play, seemed to lose his confidence after a couple of mistakes, and fell into a tie for third behind Steve Elkington and Colin Montgomerie. After rounds of 66, 65 and another 66, he shot a weak 72 on a day when others played their best. Elkington shot 64, Montgomerie 65 and Brad Faxon 63.

At Royal Lytham and St. Annes in England, in 1996, Els chased Tom Lehman through the final 18 holes of the British Open, and even though Lehman didn't play at his best, closing with 73, Ernie had made his move too late. Even with 67 he finished two strokes out of first place. Lehman won.

Suddenly, though, the World Ranking told us Els had become the best player in the game.

By winning the Open he had certainly shown formidable talent. He was 27 years old. Thirty years had passed since anyone so young had won his second Open. Jack Nicklaus was 27 in 1967 when he outscored Arnold Palmer at Baltusrol and lowered the Open's 72-hole record to 275. Nicklaus eventually won four Opens.

Els might win four as well. He seems to have everything he needs — power, finesse, a sound putting touch and steel nerves. Only a player with the best nerves and supreme confidence in his swing could have taken the dare and gone for the flagstick on the 17th in those last tense moments on Sunday. He says that inside he's boiling under the pressure, but outwardly he appears relaxed, perhaps even lethargic. It's an illusion.

"I think any player will tell you you're pretty intense. I was quite intense today, but I had confidence in my game," he said. "Other times I might feel differently. That's maybe why I've lost a couple of major championships in the last few years. Today I felt comfortable. I won't say that other times I don't feel that way, but today was different. I think that just comes with experience.

"You know, I've been playing a lot of golf the last four or five years, and I think that with experience you become a bit more

With the U.S. Open trophy and Westchester the next week, Ernie Els was proclaimed No. 1 in the world.

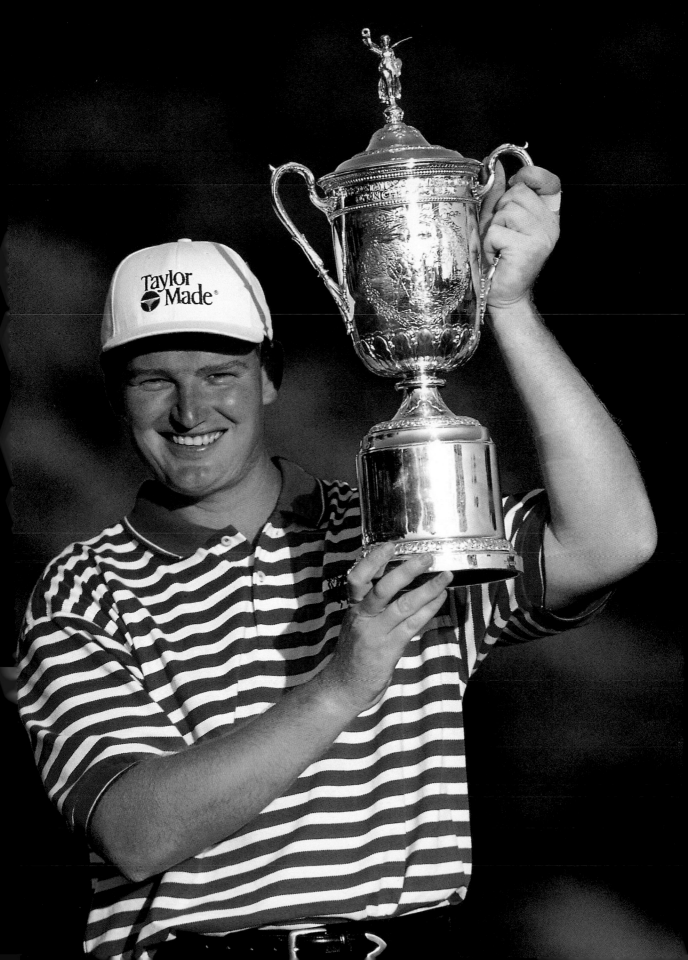

The gallery surrounding the 18th hole saluted Els when the championship was won.

calm. You have to be calm to win these kinds of tournaments. If you look at all the great players ... if you look at Jack Nicklaus, he was calm. It's hard to do that, but I'm getting closer.

"Three years ago when I won at Oakmont, it was like a war out there. I knew it was going to be the same way today, especially playing against guys like Tom Lehman and Colin Montgomerie and Jeff Maggert.

"Colin was a good guy to play with. He's such a talented player, a talented ball-striker. I knew he would play well because he's so good under pressure. I knew if I beat Colin, I would have a good chance of winning the tournament. And that's the way it turned out."

For a time, through a couple of lean years, people began to wonder about Els. He realized it and explained, "As I recall, maybe I wasn't all that patient through the last

couple of years. I've come close in other big tournaments; that went through my mind today. I didn't want to lose today. I just felt that my game was here this week and I believed in myself."

Then, with a wide grin, he said, "You know, my mom and dad are here and I just wanted to show off a little bit — show them how you win a U.S. Open."

Not long after he left Congressional, someone asked if he felt he deserved to be considered the best player in the game. He didn't argue.

"Right now, I would think so," he said. "I've never said that in my life, but, yeah, I feel I probably am. My record shows it."

Nevertheless, winning a second Open surprised him. Asked if he ever thought he would win again, he said, "To be honest, no.

"I worked hard for this one. My game's been off most of the year, but I trusted myself and my game."

Looking back to that tense afternoon, he kept thinking of the five iron on the 17th.

"That was the shot of the tournament for me," he said. "I hit a good three wood down there, as I say, and I just felt the five iron was the right club. I tend to draw my irons, hit it from right to left, and the shot just felt good for me. I felt comfortable with it. I almost holed that same shot in the morning, you know."

Asked about how often he saved par from the rough around the greens, he said, "Well, I don't think I missed too many greens."

Actually he missed 20 and hit 52. No one hit more. Of the 20 he missed, he saved par on seven and birdied two. He played well off the tee also, hitting 43 of 56 fairways, and he used just 117 putts as well, not the best — Paul Goydos had only 110 — but very good.

He said he felt badly for Montgomerie, who has come so close so often on the big occasions and hadn't won yet.

"I don't know when Colin will get his turn. I do feel for him. Believe me, I think he's a great player," Els said. "If you look at his record and the way he's playing in Europe, you know he's a great player. I know he's going to win; he just needs to stick to it."

Then, reflecting on his victory, Els described it as unbelievable. "Winning the U.S. Open doesn't come easy," he said. "A lot of guys have won one, but now I've won two. You go to a different class when you win two. You don't want to get too far ahead of yourself, but I'm very happy."

Now Els plans to savor the moment.

"It's a good feeling," he said. "It's probably going to take a while for it to sink in, but I'm really going to enjoy this one."

Els and his caddie embraced after the final putt fell for his one-stroke victory.

97th U.S. Open

June 12-15, 1997, Congressional Country Club, Bethesda, Maryland

Contestant	Rounds				Total	Prize
Ernie Els	71	67	69	69	276	$465,000.00
Colin Montgomerie	65	76	67	69	277	275,000.00
Tom Lehman	67	70	68	73	278	172,828.00
Jeff Maggert	73	66	68	74	281	120,454.00
Bob Tway	71	71	70	70	282	79,875.40
Olin Browne	71	71	69	71	282	79,875.40
Jim Furyk	74	68	69	71	282	79,875.40
Tommy Tolles	74	67	69	72	282	79,875.40
Jay Haas	73	69	68	72	282	79,875.40
Scott McCarron	73	71	69	70	283	56,949.33
Scott Hoch	71	68	72	72	283	56,949.33
David Ogrin	70	69	71	73	283	56,949.33
Loren Roberts	72	69	72	71	284	47,348.67
Stewart Cink	71	67	74	72	284	47,348.67
Billy Andrade	75	67	69	73	284	47,348.67
Bradley Hughes	75	70	71	69	285	40,086.67
Jose Maria Olazabal	71	71	72	71	285	40,086.67
Davis Love III	75	70	69	71	285	40,086.67
Nick Price	71	74	71	70	286	31,915.60
Lee Westwood	71	71	73	71	286	31,915.60
Tiger Woods	74	67	73	72	286	31,915.60
Paul Stankowski	75	70	68	73	286	31,915.60
Hal Sutton	66	73	73	74	286	31,915.60
Len Mattiace	71	75	73	68	287	24,173.50
Edward Fryatt	72	73	73	69	287	24,173.50
Scott Dunlap	75	66	75	71	287	24,173.50
Steve Elkington	75	68	72	72	287	24,173.50
Paul Goydos	73	72	74	69	288	17,443.25
Paul Azinger	72	72	74	70	288	17,443.25
Payne Stewart	71	73	73	71	288	17,443.25
Mark McNulty	67	73	75	73	288	17,443.25
Hideki Kase	68	73	73	74	288	17,443.25
Fuzzy Zoeller	72	73	69	74	288	17,443.25
Kelly Gibson	72	69	72	75	288	17,443.25
Jeff Sluman	69	72	72	75	288	17,443.25
Justin Leonard	69	72	78	70	289	13,483.14
Grant Waite	72	74	72	71	289	13,483.14
Steve Stricker	66	76	75	72	289	13,483.14
Mark O'Meara	73	73	71	72	289	13,483.14
Stuart Appleby	71	75	70	73	289	13,483.14
Frank Nobilo	71	74	70	74	289	13,483.14
John Cook	72	71	71	75	289	13,483.14
Darren Clarke	73	74	73	70	290	10,491.20
Phil Mickelson	75	68	73	74	290	10,491.20
Fred Funk	73	70	72	75	290	10,491.20
Chris Perry	70	73	71	76	290	10,491.20
Craig Parry	70	74	69	77	290	10,491.20
Jesper Parnevik	72	75	73	71	291	8,496.67
David Duval	74	73	70	74	291	8,496.67
Nick Faldo	72	74	69	76	291	8,496.67
David White	70	72	73	77	292	7,786.00
Lee Janzen	72	73	75	73	293	7,138.83
Hale Irwin	70	73	76	74	293	7,138.83

Contestant	Rounds				Total	Prize
Jack Nicklaus	73	71	75	74	293	7,138.83
Fred Couples	75	72	72	74	293	7,138.83
Peter Teravainen	71	73	74	75	293	7,138.83
Paul Broadhurst	77	69	72	75	293	7,138.83
Larry Mize	70	74	76	74	294	6,530.00
Clarence Rose	72	71	73	78	294	6,530.00
Chris Smith	77	69	74	75	295	6,270.50
Duffy Waldorf	73	73	73	76	295	6,270.50
Rodney Butcher	73	74	70	78	295	6,270.50
Steve Jones	72	75	69	79	295	6,270.50
Tom Watson	72	74	72	78	296	6,120.00
Dave Schreyer	68	73	82	74	297	6,000.00
Ben Crenshaw	73	74	76	74	297	6,000.00
Brad Faxon	72	74	76	75	297	6,000.00
Tom Kite	75	69	82	72	298	5,742.50
Mike Hulbert	73	73	77	75	298	5,742.50
Greg Kraft	77	69	76	76	298	5,742.50
John Morse	71	74	76	77	298	5,742.50
Stephen Ames	73	73	75	77	298	5,742.50
Thomas Bjorn	71	75	73	79	298	5,742.50
Jimmy Green	75	72	79	73	299	5,550.00
Randy Wylie	71	76	77	76	300	5,467.50
Andrew Coltart	74	71	76	79	300	5,467.50
Greg Towne	71	73	83	74	301	5,275.00
Dick Mast	73	69	83	76	301	5,275.00
Vijay Singh	71	76	77	77	301	5,275.00
Perry Parker	75	71	77	78	301	5,275.00
Donnie Hammond	75	71	76	79	301	5,275.00
Jack Ferenz	72	75	80	76	303	5,110.00
Marco Dawson	75	71	80	78	304	5,055.00
Slade Adams	71	74	78	83	306	5,000.00

Ronnie Black	76	72	148	Robert Allenby	75	75	150	Kent Jones	78	74	152
Lee Rinker	73	75	148	Kevin Altenhof	78	72	150	John Pillar	76	76	152
Corey Pavin	74	74	148	Ian Woosnam	76	74	150	Bob Gilder	80	73	153
Larry Rinker	76	72	148	Curtis Strange	79	71	150	Frank Lickliter	71	82	153
Paul McGinley	75	73	148	Spike McRoy	73	77	150	Peter Mitchell	75	78	153
*Joel Kribel	70	78	148	Dennis Zinkon	76	74	150	Rick Cramer	72	81	153
Bernhard Langer	73	75	148	Bill Porter	74	76	150	Dave Stockton	76	78	154
Michael Clark	77	71	148	Mark Wiebe	71	80	151	*Jason Semelsberger	78	76	154
Larry Nelson	74	75	149	Dennis Trixler	74	77	151	Roy Hunter	76	78	154
P.J. Cowan	73	76	149	*Terry Noe	75	76	151	Greg Norman	75	79	154
Mike Swartz	77	72	149	Matt Gogel	80	71	151	Brett Wayment	78	77	155
Larry Silveira	77	72	149	Mike Sposa	77	74	151	Rob Bradley	77	78	155
Ken Green	75	74	149	Anthony Aguilar	77	74	151	Roger Gunn	80	76	156
Mark Calcavecchia	73	76	149	Ken Schall	74	77	151	Ed Humenik	79	78	157
Mark Brooks	71	78	149	Russ Cochran	73	78	151	*Bob Kearney	76	81	157
*Christopher Wollmann	75	74	149	Padraig Harrington	75	76	151	Brian Tennyson	79	80	159
Mike Reid	72	77	149	Michael Bradley	77	74	151	Ted Tryba	80	79	159
Scott Simpson	76	73	149	Dan Forsman	77	74	151	Marty Schiene	81	78	159
Kenny Perry	76	73	149	Gary Robison	78	74	152	Raymond Russell	79	81	160
Sean Murphy	75	74	149	Steven Hart	74	78	152	Michael Martin	87	73	160
Jim Estes	74	75	149	Jim McGovern	72	80	152	Andrew Morse	87	77	164
John Mazza	73	76	149	Mike Brisky	70	82	152	Gregory Sweatt	78	89	167
Eric Brito	74	75	149	Jay Don Blake	79	73	152	John Daly	77		WD
Gary Nicklaus	73	77	150	Masashi Ozaki	79	73	152	David Toms	78		WD

Professionals not returning 72-hole scores received $1,000 each.   *Denotes amateur.

97th U.S. Open
Statistics

Hole	1	2	3	4	5	6	7	8	9	10	11	12	13	14	15	16	17	18	Total
Par	4	3	4	4	4	4	3	4	5	4	4	3	4	4	5	4	4	3	70

Ernie Els

	1	2	3	4	5	6	7	8	9	10	11	12	13	14	15	16	17	18	Total	
Round 1	(3)	[4]	(3)	4	4	[5]	3	(3)	5	4	4	3	4	4	5	[5]	4	[4]	71	
Round 2	4	3	(3)	4	(3)	(3)	3	4	(4)	4	[5]	3	4	4	(4)	4	[5]	3	67	
Round 3	4	[5]	4	4	4	4	3	(3)	5	[5]	4	3	4	4	(4)	(3)	(3)	3	69	
Round 4	4	3	4	4	4	[5]	(2)	(3)	[6]	(3)	4	(2)	[5]	4	5	4	4	3	69	276

Colin Montgomerie

	1	2	3	4	5	6	7	8	9	10	11	12	13	14	15	16	17	18	Total	
Round 1	4	3	4	4	4	4	(2)	4	(4)	(3)	(3)	3	(3)	4	5	(3)	[5]	3	65	
Round 2	4	[4]	4	4	4	4	3	[5]	5	[5]	4	3	4	[5]	5	[5]	[5]	3	76	
Round 3	4	3	4	(3)	4	4	(2)	(3)	(4)	[5]	4	(2)	[5]	4	5	4	[5]	(2)	67	
Round 4	(3)	3	4	4	4	[5]	(2)	4	(4)	4	4	3	4	4	5	4	[5]	3	69	277

Tom Lehman

	1	2	3	4	5	6	7	8	9	10	11	12	13	14	15	16	17	18	Total	
Round 1	4	3	[5]	(3)	4	4	3	4	5	(3)	4	3	4	4	(4)	(3)	4	3	67	
Round 2	4	[4]	[5]	4	(3)	4	3	(3)	(4)	[5]	4	3	4	(3)	5	4	4	[4]	70	
Round 3	4	3	4	(3)	(3)	[5]	(2)	4	5	[5]	[5]	3	4	(3)	5	4	4	(2)	68	
Round 4	4	3	[5]	[5]	(3)	[5]	3	(3)	5	4	4	3	4	[5]	(4)	[5]	[5]	3	73	278

○ Circled numbers represent birdies, □ squared numbers represent bogeys or double bogeys.

Hole	Yards	Par	Eagles	Birdies	Pars	Bogeys	Higher	Average
1	402	4	0	75	301	94	8	4.073
2	235	3	0	27	284	151	16	3.335
3	455	4	0	44	289	133	12	4.236
4	434	4	0	44	267	147	20	4.301
5	407	4	0	103	267	94	14	4.040
6	475	4	0	25	234	170	49	4.533
7	174	3	0	81	308	76	13	3.046
8	362	4	2	108	292	67	9	3.944
9	607	5	2	101	283	79	13	5.000
OUT	3551	35	4	608	2525	1011	154	36.508
10	466	4	0	32	235	167	44	4.479
11	415	4	0	55	331	77	15	4.109
12	187	3	0	56	317	94	11	3.126
13	461	4	0	29	275	148	26	4.368
14	439	4	0	61	267	129	21	4.234
15	583	5	1	102	276	88	11	5.013
16	441	4	0	47	272	132	27	4.299
17	480	4	0	38	258	145	37	4.406
18	190	3	0	61	331	65	21	3.105
IN	3662	35	1	481	2562	1045	213	37.139
TOTAL	7213	70	5	1089	5087	2056	367	73.647

Date	Winner	Score	Runner-Up	Venue
1895	Horace Rawlins	173 - 36 holes	Willie Dunn	Newport GC, Newport, RI
1896	James Foulis	152 - 36 holes	Horace Rawlins	Shinnecock Hills GC, Southampton, NY
1897	Joe Lloyd	162 - 36 holes	Willie Anderson	Chicago GC, Wheaton, IL
1898	Fred Herd	328 - 72 holes	Alex Smith	Myopia Hunt Club, S. Hamilton, MA
1899	Willie Smith	315	George Low Val Fitzjohn W.H. Way	Baltimore CC, Baltimore, MD
1900	Harry Vardon	313	J.H. Taylor	Chicago GC, Wheaton, IL
1901	*Willie Anderson (85)	331	Alex Smith (86)	Myopia Hunt Club, S. Hamilton, MA
1902	Laurie Auchterlonie	307	Stewart Gardner	Garden City GC, Garden City, NY
1903	*Willie Anderson (82)	307	David Brown (84)	Baltusrol GC, Springfield, NJ
1904	Willie Anderson	303	Gil Nicholls	Glen View Club, Golf, IL
1905	Willie Anderson	314	Alex Smith	Myopia Hunt Club, S. Hamilton, MA
1906	Alex Smith	295	Willie Smith	Onwentsia Club, Lake Forest, IL
1907	Alex Ross	302	Gil Nicholls	Philadelphia Cricket Club, Chestnut Hill, PA
1908	*Fred McLeod (77)	322	Willie Smith (83)	Myopia Hunt Club, S. Hamilton, MA
1909	George Sargent	290	Tom McNamara	Englewood GC, Englewood, NJ
1910	*Alex Smith (71)	298	John J. McDermott (75) Macdonald Smith (77)	Philadelphia Cricket Club, Chestnut Hill, PA
1911	*John J. McDermott (80)	307	Michael J. Brady (82) George O. Simpson (85)	Chicago GC, Wheaton, IL
1912	John J. McDermott	294	Tom McNamara	CC of Buffalo, Buffalo, NY
1913	*Francis Ouimet (72)	304	Harry Vardon (77) Edward Ray (78)	The Country Club, Brookline, MA
1914	Walter Hagen	290	Charles Evans, Jr.	Midlothian CC, Blue Island, IL
1915	Jerome D. Travers	297	Tom McNamara	Baltusrol GC, Springfield, NJ
1916	Charles Evans, Jr.	286	Jock Hutchinson	Minikahda Club, Minneapolis, MN
1917-18	No Championships Played — World War I			
1919	*Walter Hagen (77)	301	Michael J. Brady (78)	Brae Burn CC, West Newton, MA
1920	Edward Ray	295	Harry Vardon Jack Burke, Sr. Leo Diegel Jock Hutchison	Inverness Club, Toledo, OH
1921	James M. Barnes	289	Walter Hagen Fred McLeod	Columbia CC, Chevy Chase, MD
1922	Gene Sarazen	288	John L. Black Robert T. Jones, Jr.	Skokie CC, Glencoe, IL
1923	*Robert T. Jones, Jr. (76)	296	Bobby Cruickshank (78)	Inwood CC, Inwood, NY
1924	Cyril Walker	297	Robert T. Jones, Jr.	Oakland Hills CC, Birmingham, MI
1925	*William MacFarlane (147)	291	Robert T. Jones, Jr. (148)	Worcester CC, Worcester, MA
1926	Robert T. Jones, Jr.	293	Joe Turnesa	Scioto CC, Columbus, OH
1927	*Tommy Armour (76)	301	Harry Cooper (79)	Oakmont CC, Oakmont, PA
1928	*Johnny Farrell (143)	294	Robert T. Jones, Jr. (144)	Olympia Fields CC, Matteson, IL
1929	*Robert T. Jones, Jr. (141)	294	Al Espinosa (164)	Winged Foot GC, Mamaroneck, NY
1930	Robert T. Jones, Jr.	287	Macdonald Smith	Interlachen CC, Hopkins, MN

Date	Winner	Score	Runner-Up	Venue
1931	*Billy Burke (149-148)	292	George Von Elm (149-149)	Inverness Club, Toledo, OH
1932	Gene Sarazen	286	Phil Perkins	Fresh Meadows CC, Flushing, NY
			Bobby Cruickshank	
1933	Johnny Goodman	287	Ralph Guldahl	North Shore CC, Glenview, IL
1934	Olin Dutra	293	Gene Sarazen	Merion Cricket Club, Ardmore, PA
1935	Sam Parks, Jr.	299	Jimmy Thomson	Oakmont CC, Oakmont, PA
1936	Tony Manero	282	Harry Cooper	Baltusrol GC, Springfield, NJ
1937	Ralph Guldahl	281	Sam Snead	Oakland Hills CC, Birmingham, MI
1938	Ralph Guldahl	284	Dick Metz	Cherry Hills CC, Englewood, CO
1939	*Byron Nelson (68-70)	284	Craig Wood (68-73)	Philadelphia CC, West
			Denny Shute (76)	Conshohocken, PA
1940	*Lawson Little (70)	287	Gene Sarazen (73)	Canterbury GC, Cleveland, OH
1941	Craig Wood	284	Denny Shute	Colonial Club, Fort Worth, TX
1942-45	No Championships Played — World War II			
1946	*Lloyd Mangrum (72-72)	284	Vic Ghezzi (72-73)	Canterbury GC, Cleveland, OH
			Byron Nelson (72-73)	
1947	*Lew Worsham (69)	282	Sam Snead (70)	St. Louis CC, Clayton, MO
1948	Ben Hogan	276	Jimmy Demaret	Riviera CC, Los Angeles, CA
1949	Cary Middlecoff	286	Sam Snead	Medinah CC, Medinah, IL
			Clayton Heafner	
1950	*Ben Hogan (69)	287	Lloyd Mangrum (73)	Merion GC, Ardmore, PA
			George Fazio (75)	
1951	Ben Hogan	287	Clayton Heafner	Oakland Hills CC, Birmingham, MI
1952	Julius Boros	281	Ed (Porky) Oliver	Northwood CC, Dallas, TX
1953	Ben Hogan	283	Sam Snead	Oakmont CC, Oakmont, PA
1954	Ed Furgol	284	Gene Littler	Baltusrol GC, Springfield, NJ
1955	*Jack Fleck (69)	287	Ben Hogan (72)	The Olympic Club, San Francisco, CA
1956	Cary Middlecoff	281	Ben Hogan	Oak Hill CC, Rochester, NY
			Julius Boros	
1957	*Dick Mayer (72)	282	Cary Middlecoff (79)	Inverness Club, Toledo, OH
1958	Tommy Bolt	283	Gary Player	Southern Hills CC, Tulsa, OK
1959	Billy Casper	282	Bob Rosburg	Winged Foot GC, Mamaroneck, NY
1960	Arnold Palmer	280	Jack Nicklaus	Cherry Hills CC, Englewood, CO
1961	Gene Littler	281	Bob Goalby	Oakland Hills CC, Birmingham, MI
			Doug Sanders	
1962	*Jack Nicklaus (71)	283	Arnold Palmer (74)	Oakmont CC, Oakmont, PA
1963	*Julius Boros (70)	293	Jacky Cupit (73)	The Country Club, Brookline, MA
			Arnold Palmer (76)	
1964	Ken Venturi	278	Tommy Jacobs	Congressional CC, Bethesda, MD
1965	*Gary Player (71)	282	Kel Nagle (74)	Bellerive CC, St. Louis, MO
1966	*Billy Casper (69)	278	Arnold Palmer (73)	The Olympic Club, San Francisco, CA
1967	Jack Nicklaus	275	Arnold Palmer	Baltusrol GC, Springfield, NJ
1968	Lee Trevino	275	Jack Nicklaus	Oak Hill CC, Rochester, NY
1969	Orville Moody	281	Deane Beman	Champions GC, Houston, TX
			Al Geiberger	
			Bob Rosburg	
1970	Tony Jacklin	281	Dave Hill	Hazeltine National GC, Chaska, MN
1971	*Lee Trevino (68)	280	Jack Nicklaus (71)	Merion GC, Ardmore, PA
1972	Jack Nicklaus	290	Bruce Crampton	Pebble Beach GL, Pebble Beach, CA
1973	Johnny Miller	279	John Schlee	Oakmont CC, Oakmont, PA
1974	Hale Irwin	287	Forrest Fezler	Winged Foot GC, Mamaroneck, NY
1975	*Lou Graham (71)	287	John Mahaffey (73)	Medinah CC, Medinah, IL
1976	Jerry Pate	277	Tom Weiskopf	Atlanta Athletic Club, Duluth, GA
			Al Geiberger	

Date	Winner	Score	Runner-Up	Venue
1977	Hubert Green	278	Lou Graham	Southern Hills CC, Tulsa, OK
1978	Andy North	285	Dave Stockton J.C. Snead	Cherry Hills CC, Englewood, CO
1979	Hale Irwin	284	Gary Player Jerry Pate	Inverness Club, Toledo, OH
1980	Jack Nicklaus	272	Isao Aoki	Baltusrol GC, Springfield, NJ
1981	David Graham	273	George Burns Bill Rogers	Merion GC, Ardmore, PA
1982	Tom Watson	282	Jack Nicklaus	Pebble Beach GL, Pebble Beach, CA
1983	Larry Nelson	280	Tom Watson	Oakmont CC, Oakmont, PA
1984	*Fuzzy Zoeller (67)	276	Greg Norman (75)	Winged Foot GC, Mamaroneck, NY
1985	Andy North	279	Dave Barr Chen Tze Chung Denis Watson	Oakland Hills CC, Birmingham, MI
1986	Raymond Floyd	279	Lanny Wadkins Chip Beck	Shinnecock Hills GC, Southampton, NY
1987	Scott Simpson	277	Tom Watson	The Olympic Club, San Francisco, CA
1988	*Curtis Strange (71)	278	Nick Faldo (75)	The Country Club, Brookline, MA
1989	Curtis Strange	278	Chip Beck Mark McCumber Ian Woosnam	Oak Hill CC, Rochester, NY
1990	*Hale Irwin (74+3)	280	Mike Donald (74+4)	Medinah CC, Medinah, IL
1991	*Payne Stewart (75)	282	Scott Simpson (77)	Hazeltine National GC, Chaska, MN
1992	Tom Kite	285	Jeff Sluman	Pebble Beach GL, Pebble Beach, CA
1993	Lee Janzen	272	Payne Stewart	Baltusrol GC, Springfield, NJ
1994	*Ernie Els (74+4+4)	289	Loren Roberts (74+4+5) Colin Montgomerie (78)	Oakmont CC, Oakmont, PA
1995	Corey Pavin	280	Greg Norman	Shinnecock Hills GC, Southampton, NY
1996	Steve Jones	278	Tom Lehman Davis Love III	Oakland Hills CC, Birmingham, MI
1997	Ernie Els	276	Colin Montgomerie	Congressional CC, Bethesda, MD

Oldest champion (years/months/days)
45/0/15 — Hale Irwin (1990)

Youngest champion
19/10/14 — John J. McDermott (1911)

Most victories
4 — Willie Anderson (1901, '03, '04, '05)
4 — Robert T. Jones, Jr. (1923, '26, '29, '30)
4 — Ben Hogan (1948, '50, '51, '53)
4 — Jack Nicklaus (1962, '67, '72, '80)
3 — Hale Irwin (1974, '79, '90)
2 — by 11 players: Alex Smith (1906, '10), John J. McDermott (1911, '12), Walter Hagen (1914, '19), Gene Sarazen (1922, '32), Ralph Guldahl (1937, '38), Cary Middlecoff (1949, '56), Julius Boros (1952, '63), Billy Casper (1959, '66), Lee Trevino (1968, '71), Andy North (1978, '85), and Curtis Strange (1988, '89).

Consecutive victories
Willie Anderson (1903, '04, '05)
John J. McDermott (1911, '12)
Robert T. Jones, Jr. (1929, '30)
Ralph Guldahl (1937, '38)
Ben Hogan (1950, '51)
Curtis Strange (1988, '89)

Most times runner-up
4 — Sam Snead
4 — Robert T. Jones, Jr.
4 — Arnold Palmer
4 — Jack Nicklaus

Longest course
7,213 yards — Congressional CC, Bethesda, MD (1997)

Shortest course
Since World War II
6,528 yards — Merion GC (East Course), Ardmore, PA (1971, '81)

Most often host club of Open
7 — Baltusrol GC, Springfield, NJ (1903, '15, '36, '54, '67, '80, '93)
7 — Oakmont (PA) CC (1927, '35, '53, '62, '73, '83, '94)

Largest entry
6,244 (1992)

Smallest entry
11 (1895)

Lowest score, 72 holes
272 — Jack Nicklaus (63-71-70-68), at Baltusrol GC (Lower Course), Springfield, NJ (1980)
272 — Lee Janzen (67-67-69-69), at Baltusrol GC (Lower Course), Springfield, NJ (1993)

Lowest score, first 54 holes
203 — George Burns (69-66-68), at Merion GC (East Course), Ardmore, PA (1981)
203 — Tze-Chung Chen (65-69-69), at Oakland

Hills CC (South Course), Birmingham, MI (1985)
203 — Lee Janzen (67-67-69), at Baltusrol GC (Lower Course), Springfield, NJ (1993)

Lowest score, last 54 holes
203 — Loren Roberts (69-64-70), at Oakmont CC, Oakmont, PA (1994)

Lowest score, first 36 holes
134 — Jack Nicklaus (63-71), at Baltusrol GC (Lower Course), Springfield, NJ (1980)
134 — Chen Tze-Chung (65-69), at Oakland Hills CC (South Course), Birmingham, MI (1985)
134 — Lee Janzen (67-67), at Baltusrol GC (Lower Course), Springfield, NJ (1993)

Lowest score, last 36 holes
132 — Larry Nelson (65-67), at Oakmont CC, Oakmont, PA (1983)

Lowest score, 9 holes
29 — Neal Lancaster (second nine, fourth round) at Shinnecock Hills GC, Southampton, NY (1995)
29 — Neal Lancaster (second nine, second round) at Oakland Hills CC, Birmingham, MI (1996)

Lowest score, 18 holes
63 — Johnny Miller, fourth round at Oakmont CC, Oakmont, PA (1973)
63 — Jack Nicklaus, first round at Baltusrol GC (Lower Course), Springfield, NJ (1980)
63 — Tom Weiskopf, first round at Baltusrol GC (Lower Course), Springfield, NJ (1980)

Largest winning margin
11 — Willie Smith (315), at Baltimore (MD) CC (Roland Park Course) (1899)

Highest winning score
Since World War II
293 — Julius Boros, at The Country Club, Brookline, MA (1963) (won in playoff)

Best start by champion
63 — Jack Nicklaus, at Baltusrol GC (Lower Course), Springfield, NJ (1980)

Best finish by champion
63 — Johnny Miller, at Oakmont (PA) CC (1973)

Worst start by champion
Since World War II
76 — Ben Hogan, at Oakland Hills CC (South Course), Birmingham, MI (1951)
76 — Jack Fleck, at The Olympic Club (Lake Course), San Francisco, CA (1955)

Worst finish by champion
Since World War II
75 — Cary Middlecoff, at Medinah CC (No. 3 Course), Medinah, IL (1949)
75 — Hale Irwin, at Inverness Club, Toledo, OH (1979)

Lowest score to lead field, 18 holes
  63 — Jack Nicklaus and Tom Weiskopf, at
    Baltusrol GC (Lower Course), Springfield,
    NJ (1980)
Lowest score to lead field, 36 holes
  134 — Jack Nicklaus (63-71), at Baltusrol GC
    (Lower Course), Springfield, NJ (1980)
  134 — Chen Tze-Chung (65-69), at Oakland
    Hills CC (South Course), Birmingham, MI
    (1985)
  134 — Lee Janzen (67-67), at Baltusrol GC
    (Lower Course), Springfield, NJ (1993)
Lowest score to lead field, 54 holes
  203 — George Burns (69-66-68), at Merion GC
    (East Course), Ardmore, PA (1981)
  203 — Chen Tze-Chung (65-69-69), at Oakland
    Hills CC (South Course), Birmingham, MI
    (1985)
  203 — Lee Janzen (67-67-69), at Baltusrol GC
    (Lower Course), Springfield, NJ (1993)
Highest score to lead field, 18 holes
  Since World War II
  71 — Sam Snead, at Oakland Hills CC (South
    Course), Birmingham, MI (1951)
  71 — Tommy Bolt, Julius Boros, and Dick
    Metz, at Southern Hills CC, Tulsa, OK
    (1958)
  71 — Tony Jacklin, at Hazeltine National GC,
    Chaska, MN (1970)
  71 — Orville Moody, Jack Nicklaus, Chi Chi
    Rodriguez, Mason Rudolph, Tom Shaw,
    and Kermit Zarley, at Pebble Beach (CA)
    Golf Links (1972)
Highest score to lead field, 36 holes
  Since World War II
  144 — Bobby Locke (73-71), at Oakland Hills
    CC (South Course), Birmingham, MI
    (1951)
  144 — Tommy Bolt (67 77) and E. Harvie
    Ward (74-70), at The Olympic Club (Lake
    Course), San Francisco, CA (1955)
  144 — Homero Blancas (74-70), Bruce
    Crampton (74-70), Jack Nicklaus (71-73),
    Cesar Seduno (72-72), Lanny Wadkins
    (76-68) and Kermit Zarley (71-73), at
    Pebble Beach (CA) Golf Links (1972)
Highest score to lead field, 54 holes
  Since World War II
  218 — Bobby Locke (73-71-74), at Oakland
    Hills CC (South Course), Birmingham, MI
    (1951)
  218 — Jacky Cupit (70-72-76), at The Country
    Club, Brookline, MA (1963)
Highest 36-hole cut
  155 — at The Olympic Club (Lakeside
    Course), San Francisco, CA (1955)
Most players to tie for lead, 18 holes
  7 — at Pebble Beach (CA) Golf Links (1972);

at Southern Hills CC, Tulsa, OK (1977);
    and at Shinnecock Hills GC,
    Southampton, NY (1896)
Most players to tie for lead, 36 holes
  6 — at Pebble Beach (CA) Golf Links (1972)
Most players to tie for lead, 54 holes
  4 — at Oakmont (PA) CC (1973)
Most sub-par rounds, championship
  124 — at Medinah CC (No. 3 Course),
    Medinah, IL (1990)
Most sub-par 72-hole totals, championship
  28 — at Medinah CC (No. 3 Course),
    Medinah, IL (1990)
Most sub-par scores, first round
  39 — at Medinah CC (No. 3 Course),
    Medinah, IL (1990)
Most sub-par scores, second round
  47 — at Medinah CC (No. 3 Course),
    Medinah, IL (1990)
Most sub-par scores, third round
  24 — at Medinah CC (No. 3 Course),
    Medinah, IL (1990)
Most sub-par scores, fourth round
  18 — at Baltusrol GC (Lower Course),
    Springfield, NJ (1993)
Most sub-par rounds by one player in one
championship
  4 — Billy Casper, at The Olympic Club
    (Lakeside Course), San Francisco, CA
    (1966)
  4 — Lee Trevino, at Oak Hill CC (East
    Course), Rochester, NY (1968)
  4 — Tony Jacklin, at Hazeltine National GC,
    Chaska, MN (1970)
  4 — Lee Janzen, at Baltusrol GC (Lower
    Course), Springfield, NJ (1993)
Highest score, one hole
  19 — Ray Ainsley, at the 16th (par 4) at
    Cherry Hills CC, Englewood, CO (1938)
Most consecutive birdies
  6 — George Burns (holes 2–7), at Pebble
    Beach (CA) Golf Links (1972) and Andy
    Dillard (holes 1-6), at Pebble Beach (CA)
    Golf Links (1992)
Most consecutive 3s
  7 — Hubert Green (holes 10–16), at Southern
    Hills Country Club, Tulsa, OK (1977)
  7 — Peter Jacobsen (holes 1–7), at The
    Country Club, Brookline, MA (1988)
Most consecutive Opens
  41 — Jack Nicklaus (1957-97)
Most Opens completed 72 holes
  34 — Jack Nicklaus
Most consecutive Opens completed 72 holes
  22 — Walter Hagen (1913-36; no Champion-
    ships 1917-18)
  22 — Gene Sarazen (1920-41)
  22 — Gary Player (1958-79)

Robert Sommers is the former editor and publisher of the USGA's *Golf Journal*, author of *The U.S. Open: Golf's Ultimate Challenge* and *Golf Anecdotes*, and is based in Port St. Lucie, Florida.

Michael Cohen is a photographer based in New York City and a contributor to many magazines and books.

Fred Vuich is a staff photographer for *Golf Magazine*, a contributor to many books, and is based in Pittsburgh.

97th U.S. Open Championship
Congressional Country Club
June 12-15, 1997